Exploring CANADA

with the FIVE Themes of Geography

by Nancy Golden

The Rosen Publishing Group's
PowerKids Press™
New York

Published in 2005 by The Rosen Publishing Group, Inc.
29 East 21st Street, New York, NY 10010

First Edition

Editor: Geeta Sobha
Book Design: Michelle Innes

Photo Credits: Cover, p. 1 © Darwin Wiggett/Corbis; p. 9 © Rich Reid/National Geographic Image Collection; pp. 9 (Jasper National Park, Alberta), 15 (lumberjack), 16, 19 (St. Lawrence) © Paul A. Souders/Corbis; p. 10 © Wayne R. Bilenduke/Getty Images; p. 10 (moose) © Art Wolfe/Getty Images; p. 12 © Paul Thompson/Eye Ubiquitous/Corbis; p. 12 (Gretzky) © Neal Preston/Corbis; p. 15 © Photodisc/Getty Images; p. 19 © Raymond Gehman/Corbis; p. 21 © Randy Olsen/National Geographic Image Collection

Library of Congress Cataloging-in-Publication Data

Golden, Nancy.
    Exploring Canada with the five themes of geography / by Nancy
Golden.— 1st ed.
    p. cm. — (Library of the Western Hemisphere)
    Includes index.
    Contents: The five themes of geography — Location — Place —
Human-environment interaction — Movement — Regions — Fact zone.
    ISBN 1-4042-2669-9 (lib. bdg.) — ISBN 0-8239-4629-0 (pbk.)
    1. Canada—Geography—Juvenile literature. [1. Canada—Geography.] I.
Title. II. Series.

F1011.3.G65 2005
917.1—dc22

                                        2003019261

Manufactured in the United States of America

Contents

The Five Themes of Geography 4

1 Location 6

2 Place 8

3 Human-Environment Interaction 14

4 Movement 18

5 Regions 20

Fact Zone 22

Glossary 23

Index 24

Web Sites 24

Geographers study places on Earth, such as Canada, by looking at the area's climate, resources, people, and physical features. One way to organize and understand all this information is by using the five themes of geography: location, place, human-environment interaction, movement, and regions. Let's use these five themes of geography to learn about Canada, the second largest country in the world.

1 Location

Where is Canada?

By looking at Canada's absolute, or exact, location, we can define exactly where it is in the world. We do this by using the imaginary lines of longitude and latitude.

Another way to define Canada's location is by using its relative, or general, location. Identifying the countries near Canada is one way of learning its relative location. Another way to describe Canada's relative location is by using its cardinal points—east, west, north, and south.

2 Place

What is Canada like?

By looking at Canada's physical and human features, we can get to know its land and people. Landforms, bodies of water, climate, and plant and animal life are all examples of physical features. Human features are things, such as buildings, cities, traditions, and government, that people have created.

3 Human-Environment Interaction

How do the people and the environment of Canada affect each other?

This theme explains the relationship between people and their environment. It answers two questions: How have people adapted, or changed, to suit their environment? and How has the environment been changed by people?

4 Movement

How do people, goods, and ideas get from place to place in Canada?

Movement happens within Canada as well as from Canada to other areas of the world. Transportation of Canada's people, goods, and ideas is explained in this theme.

5 Regions

What does Canada have in common with other places around the world? What features do places within Canada share to make them part of a region?

To define a place as a part of a region, we group it with other places that share similar features. The features can be physical or cultural, including landforms, types of government, and language.

Canada's absolute location is 60° north and 95° west. Canada's relative location can be found by defining the areas around it. Canada shares its entire southern border with the United States. The U.S. state of Alaska and the Pacific Ocean border Canada to the west. Canada stretches east to the Atlantic Ocean and north to the Arctic Ocean. Canada takes up the northern portion of North America.

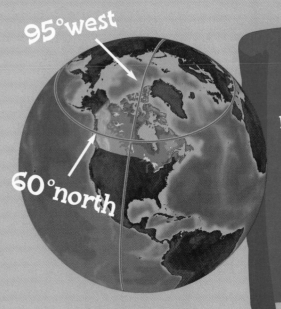

95°west

60°north

Where in the World?

Absolute location is the point where the lines of longitude and latitude meet.

Longitude tells a place's position in degrees east or west of the prime meridian, a line that runs through Greenwich, London.

Latitude tells a place's position in degrees north or south of the equator, the imaginary line that goes around the middle of the earth.

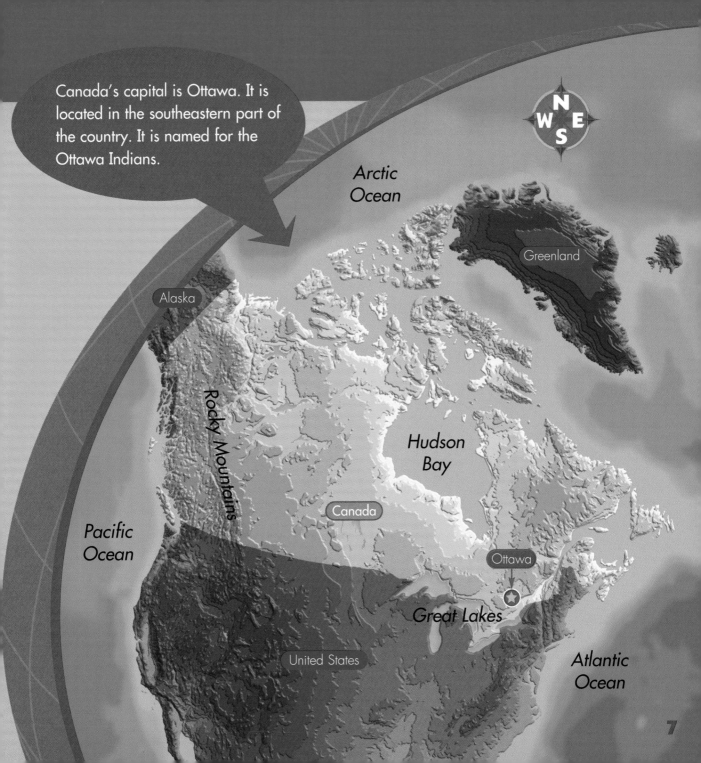

Canada's capital is Ottawa. It is located in the southeastern part of the country. It is named for the Ottawa Indians.

Arctic Ocean

Greenland

Alaska

Rocky Mountains

Hudson Bay

Canada

Pacific Ocean

Ottawa

Great Lakes

United States

Atlantic Ocean

N
W   E
S

Physical Features

Canada is the second largest country in the world. Most of Canada is part of the Canadian Shield, an area covered by rocky land. In the far northern regions is tundra, which is flat, frozen land with little or no trees. The Canadian Cordillera in the west is made up of fertile valleys and the Rocky Mountains. Forests of pine, spruce, cedar, and other trees cover the Rocky Mountains. Between the Cordillera and the Canadian Shield lie the Interior Plains, which is made up of both hills and flat grassland. The Great Lakes and St. Lawrence Lowlands is an area of flat plains. Along Canada's coastlines are many islands. Canada has about three million lakes. The lakes are often connected to each other by streams and rivers.

The area of Jasper National Park includes part of the Rocky Mountains. The park is home to many kinds of wildlife and plant life.

Alberta is one of Canada's three Prairie Provinces.

Tundra plant life include lichens, mosses, and small shrubs.

9

Moose live in the northern forests of Canada. They grow to about 6½ feet tall. The males can be identified by their antlers.

Polar Bear National Park is in Ontario, Canada. It is home to polar bears and many other animals, such as seals, walrus, and black bears.

10

Canada's climate is as varied as its land. Temperatures in the far northern sections are extremely cold. In the southern regions, the summers are hot and the winters are very cold.

Canada is home to many types of mammals and birds. Polar bears, seals, snowy owls, caribou, and ptarmigans can be found in the tundra region. In the northern forests, beavers, black bears, blue jays, and ravens can be found. In the Rocky Mountains, there are elk, goats, and mule deer. Canada's waters are home to whales, otters, and many types of fish. Reptiles and insects are mainly found in the far south.

Human Features

There are over 32 million people living in Canada. Most Canadians live in the southern part of the country.

Canada's CN tower, in Toronto, is the tallest building in the world. It is 1,815 ft. 5 in. (533.33 meters) tall.

Hockey is a large part of Canadian culture. Former hockey player Wayne Gretzky is world famous.

About one-third of the people live in the three largest cities: Toronto, Montreal, and Vancouver. The Inuit, one of Canada's native peoples, live in the far north.

Canada was colonized by both England and France. Therefore, both English and French are official languages of Canada. The population of Canada includes people from all over the world, especially Southeast Asia and Latin America. Canadian culture remains heavily influenced by its European settlers. However, immigrants tend to keep the cultural practices of their home countries.

A major part of Canadian culture is sports such as ice hockey and lacrosse. Both of these sports come from the native Indians of Canada.

Canada's national government is run by the Parliament. The leader is called the prime minister.

Canada's environment determines where people live. Very few people live in the northern part of the country. The weather there is so cold that the land is frozen, making farming and even building homes difficult. The St. Lawrence Lowlands, known as Canada's heartland, is home to two-thirds of the country's population.

Canada has a great wealth of natural resources. These include timber, water, petroleum, natural gas, iron ore, and fish. Canadians use these resources to meet their needs.

Canada has many fast-moving rivers. Dams have been built to turn the power of these rivers into energy. This energy is called hydroelectricity. It is a form of electricity that does not pollute the environment.

Like other places around the world, Canada's environment is threatened by pollution. Pollution is a

Forests cover almost one-half of Canada's land. In British Columbia, northern Ontario, Québec, and the northern Prairie Provinces, timber production is important.

Dams are not just power sources. The Oldman Dam in southern Alberta provides water for farming.

Wheat is Canada's most important crop. Alberta, Manitoba, and Saskatchewan together are among the largest wheat growers in the world.

Mining nickel has polluted this area in Ontario. This type of pollution happens when nickel is removed from its surrounding rock.

result of human activity. Motor vehicles are the number one cause of air pollution. Air pollution can be serious around cities and major manufacturing areas. Many of Canada's major waterways have been polluted by waste from factories and farming.

Although building dams creates hydroelectricity, it also has negative effects. Large areas of land are flooded. This can destroy important natural habitats, endangering the animals that live in those habitats.

Canadians are trying to preserve their natural resources. They have created many national parks in which trees, animals, and the land are protected. They are educating the public about pollution. Events like Clean Air Day are encouraging Canadians to care about the environment.

4 Movement

Canada's transportation system is important to moving people and goods across the country. Canada's main river, the St. Lawrence, connects the Great Lakes to the Atlantic Ocean. It is one of North America's most important routes for shipping goods. Canada also has two major airlines and about 700 small airlines. These small airlines go places where other transportation cannot. The Trans-Canada Highway is a roadway that stretches from the east all the way to the west coast.

Canada shares news and information across the country through its newspapers, television and radio stations, and Internet providers.

Canada and the United States not only share a border, they have also always shared information and culture. This is done through television, radio, newspapers, and travel back and forth between the countries.

Ferries move people across rivers such as the St. Lawrence in Canada.

The Trans-Canada Highway is the world's longest national road. It passes through Canada's 10 provinces.

Canada is divided into 10 provinces and three territories that are run by the government. Canada's capital city, Ottawa, is located in the province of Ontario.

Canada is part of the Commonwealth of Nations. This is made up of countries that once belonged to England. Australia, South Africa, and India are also members.

Canada can also be thought of in terms of geographical regions. Canada is a part of the North American continent. The physical regions within Canada are based on the kinds of land, such as the Lowlands and the Canadian Shield. Canada's three territories, the Yukon Territory, Northwest Territory, and Nunavut Territory, make up about one-third of Canada's land.

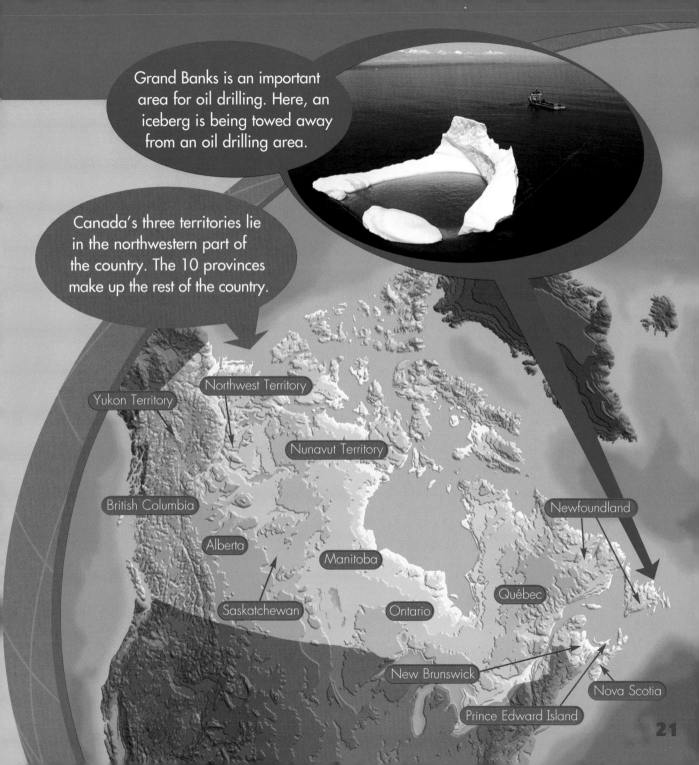

Grand Banks is an important area for oil drilling. Here, an iceberg is being towed away from an oil drilling area.

Canada's three territories lie in the northwestern part of the country. The 10 provinces make up the rest of the country.

Yukon Territory

Northwest Territory

Nunavut Territory

British Columbia

Newfoundland

Alberta

Manitoba

Saskatchewan

Ontario

Québec

New Brunswick

Nova Scotia

Prince Edward Island

21

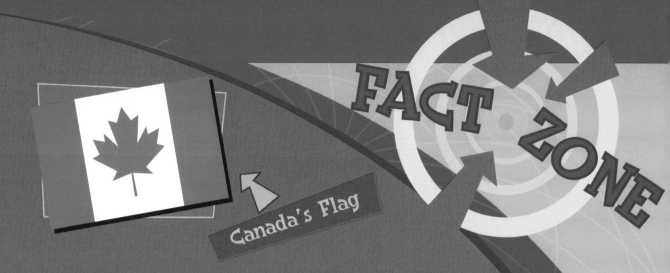

Canada's Flag

Population (2003) 32,207,113

Languages English and French

Absolute location 60° north, 95° west

Capital city Ottawa

Area 3,849,674 square miles
(9,970,610 square kilometers)

Highest point Mount Logan,
3.7 miles (5,959 meters)

Lowest point Atlantic Ocean,
zero meters

Land boundaries United States

Natural resources timber, water,
petroleum, natural gas, iron ore,
and fish

Agricultural products
wheat, canola, vegetables, barley,
maize, potatoes, fruits, tobacco,
soybeans, and livestock

Major exports motor vehicles and
parts, industrial machinery, aircraft,
telecommunications equipment,
chemicals, plastics, fertilizers, wood
pulp, timber, crude petroleum, natural
gas, electricity, and aluminum

Major imports machinery and equipment, motor vehicles and parts, crude
oil, chemicals, and electricity

Glossary

culture (KUHL-chur) The way of life, ideas, customs, and traditions shared by a group of people.

environment (en-VYE-ruhn-muhnt) The natural world of the land, sea, and air.

fertile (FUR-tuhl) Able to grow plenty of plants.

habitat (HAB-uh-tat) The place and natural conditions in which a plant or animal lives.

hemisphere (HEM-uhss-fihr) One half of the earth.

hydroelectricity (hye-droh-i-lek-TRISS-uh-tee) Electricity produced by water power that turns a generator.

interaction (in-tur-AK-shuhn) The action between people, groups, or things.

lichen (LYE-ken) A flat, mosslike growth.

ore (OR) Rock thats contains metal, such as iron.

province (PROV-uhnss) A district or region of some countries.

region (REE-juhn) An area or a district.

resource (RI-sorss) Something valuable or useful to a place or person.

shrub (SHRUHB) A bush or plant with stems that are close to the ground.

Index

A
Arctic Ocean, 6
Atlantic Ocean, 6, 18

C
Canadian Cordillera, 8
Canadian Shield, 8, 20
climate, 4, 11
Commonwealth of
  Nations, 20
culture, 13, 18

E
environment, 14, 17

F
fertile, 8

G
Great Lakes, 8, 18

H
hydroelectricity, 14, 17

I
ice hockey, 13
islands, 8

L
lacrosse, 13
lakes, 8

N
Northwest Territory, 20
Nunavut Territory, 20

O
Ontario, 20
Ottawa, 20

P
Pacific Ocean, 6
pollution, 14, 17
provinces, 20

R
regions, 4, 8, 11, 20
resources, 4, 14, 17
Rocky Mountains, 8, 11

S
St. Lawrence Lowlands,
  8, 14
St. Lawrence, 18

T
Trans-Canada Highway,
  18
transportation, 18

W
waterways, 17

Y
Yukon Territory, 20

Web Sites

Due to the changing nature of Internet links, PowerKids Press has developed
an on-line list of Web sites related to the subject of this book. This site is
updated regularly. Please use this link to access the list:
http://www.powerkidslinks.com/lwh/canada/